American Government Today

WASHINGTON, D.C.

By Mark Sanders

Raintree Steck-Vaughn Publishers
A Harcourt Company

Austin · New York
www.steck-vaughn.com

Published by Raintree Steck-Vaughn Publishers,
an imprint of Steck-Vaughn Company

Library of Congress Cataloging-in-Publication Data
Sanders, Mark.
    Washington, D.C. / Mark Sanders
        p. cm.—(American government today)
    Includes index.
    ISBN 0-7398-1789-2
        1. Washington (D.C.)—Juvenile literature. 2. Washington (D.C.)—
    History—Juvenile literature. 3. Washington (D.C.)—Buildings, structures,
    etc.—Juvenile literature. [1. Washington (D.C.)] I. Title. II. Series.
    F194.3 .S26 2000
    975.3—dc21   00-030773

Printed in the United States of America
10 9 8 7 6 5 4 3 2 1 W 03 02 01 00

Photo Acknowledgments
Cover ©UNIPHOTO Picture Agency; p.4 ©AP/Wide World Photos; p.7 ©North Wind
Pictures; p.16 ©FPG International/Vladimir Pcholkin; p.28 ©George Gibbons/FPG
International; p.29 ©Bill Clark/Courtesy of National Park Service, National Capital Region
and Parks & History Association; p.31 ©Courtesy United States Holocaust Memorial
Museum; p.32 ©Corbis; p.33 ©Bill Clark/Courtesy of National Park Service, National
Capital Region and Parks & History Association; p.34 ©Robert Shafer/Tony Stone
Worldwide; p.37 ©AP/Wide World Photos; p.40 ©Chuck Wasson, Courtesy Parks &
History Association 1998.

Additional Photography by Photodisc and Corbis

CONTENTS

THE CITY AND HOW IT CAME TO BE

The capital of the United States is Washington, D.C. It is located at the center of the original 13 states along the Atlantic coast. It is also known as the District of Columbia. The country's founders wanted a capital that was not in the North. Nor could it be in the South. It was important to keep everyone happy. So part of the land that makes up Washington, D.C., came from Maryland, a northern state. The rest came from Virginia, a southern state.

The place for the nation's capital was chosen in 1790 by a group of people appointed by President George Washington. Before a decision was made to create a special place for the capital, several cities briefly served as the nation's capital. They included Philadelphia, Pennsylvania; Trenton, New Jersey; Annapolis, Maryland; and New York City.

Crowds jam the Mall, from the Washington Monument to the Capitol.

On July 16, 1790, Congress approved a federal district to be the home of the nation's government. The city was not to be more than a square 10 miles (16 km) on each side. This is the same as 100 square miles (259 sq km).

Washington, D.C. is in the shape of a diamond. It is situated on the Potomac River. The river separates Washington, D.C., from Virginia. Virginia had given some land, but it was never used. That land was later returned to Virginia. It now includes the cities of Arlington and Alexandria. Today Washington, D.C., is made up of 69 square miles (178 sq km).

The city was named in honor of the country's first president, George Washington. At first, Washington wanted to call the capital Federal City. But George Washington was a well-liked person. So the city was named after him. The District of Columbia takes its name from the explorer Christopher Columbus.

An early map of the District of Columbia

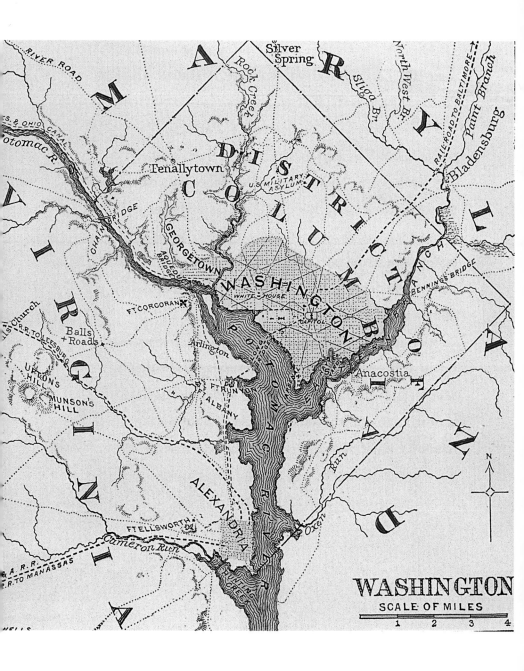

MARYLAND

VIRGINIA

DISTRICT OF COLUMBIA

Silver Spring

River Road

Rock Creek

Sliga Br.

North West Br.

RAIL ROAD TO BALTIMORE

Paint Branch

Bladensburg

C. & OHIO CANAL

Potomac R.

Tenallytown

U.S. MILITARY ASYLUM

CHAIN BRIDGE

GEORGETOWN

AQUEDUCT BRIDGE

WASHINGTON

WHITE HOUSE

CAPITOL

FT. CORCORAN

BENNINGS BRIDGE

EAST BRANCH

Balls + Roads

Arlington

UPTON'S HILL

MUNSON'S HILL

FALLS CHURCH

R.R. TO LEESBURG

FT. RUN ALBANY

Anacostia

POTOMAC RIVER

EASTERN BRANCH

Oxen Run

ALEXANDRIA

FT. ELLSWORTH

Cameron Run

R.R. TO MANASSAS

& A.R.R.

KING CREEK

WELLS

N

WASHINGTON

SCALE OF MILES

1   2   3   4

7 ★

Much of the District is flat land, with most of it less than 100 feet (30 m) above sea level. Mount St. Alban, in the Northwest, is the highest part.

Washington, D.C., is the home of the U.S. government. Washington, D.C., is also home to nearly 600,000 people. About 70 percent of the city's population is African American. Both the Asian and Hispanic populations are growing. Today, almost 4.65 million people live in the area around Washington, D.C. This includes not only the city of Washington, but also parts of Maryland and Virginia.

Between 200,000 and 300,000 people are employed by the U.S. government, Washington's largest industry. The second largest industry is the tourist business. Each year more than 20 million visitors come to tour the nation's capital. Because so many people visit the city, there are many hotels, restaurants, and stores.

A WELL-PLANNED CAPITAL CITY

From the beginning, Washington, D.C., was planned with an eye to the future. It has wide, tree-lined streets. It has big buildings and monuments. Monuments are objects built as reminders of someone or some event. They may also be known as landmarks, which are important buildings or places.

The city is laid out in a simple grid. There are four areas, all beginning at the Capitol. These are Northwest, Northeast, Southwest, and Southeast.

For its first hundred years, Washington grew slowly. Originally it was a small town where animals roamed the unpaved streets. In 1840 there were only 23,000 people living there. On the other hand, New York City already had 400,000 residents. By 1860 the population of the city was around 61,000. In the next 25 years, the population more than tripled.

A Map of Washington D.C.

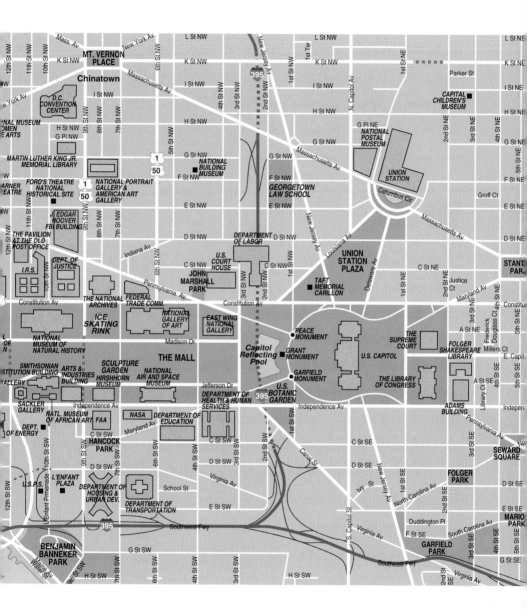

Mass. Av
New York Av
L St NW
L St NW
L St NE
12th St NW
11th St NW
10th St NW
MT. VERNON PLACE
K St NW
K St NW
Parker St
K St NE
K St NW
Chinatown
Massachusetts Av
395
1st Ter
1st St NE
6th St NW
I St NW
I St NW
I St NW
I St NW
CAPITAL CHILDREN'S MUSEUM
I St NE
York Av
D.C. CONVENTION CENTER
H St NW
H St NW
H St NW
H St NW
NATIONAL MUSEUM WOMEN ARTS
H St NW
9th St NW
8th St NW
7th St NW
G Pl NW
G St NW
G St NW
G Pl NE
NATIONAL POSTAL MUSEUM
2nd St NE
3rd St NE
4th St NE
5th St NE
G St NE
MARTIN LUTHER KING JR. MEMORIAL LIBRARY
5th St NW
1
50
G St NW
NATIONAL BUILDING MUSEUM
G St NW
UNION STATION
F St NE
F St NW
F St NW
WARNER THEATRE
FORD'S THEATRE NATIONAL HISTORICAL SITE
1
50
NATIONAL PORTRAIT GALLERY & AMERICAN ART GALLERY
8th St NW
7th St NW
E St NW
GEORGETOWN LAW SCHOOL
Columbus Cir
Groff Ct
E St NE
E St NW
Massachusetts Av
D St NE
THE PAVILION AT THE OLD POST OFFICE
J EDGAR HOOVER FBI BUILDING
7th St NW
D St NW
DEPARTMENT OF LABOR
D St NW
New Jersey Av
Louisiana Av
UNION STATION PLAZA
STANT PAR
12th St NW
Indiana Av
C St NW
U.S. COURT HOUSE
3rd St NW
2nd St NW
C St NW
C St NE
C St NE
Maryland Av
DEPT OF JUSTICE
6th St NW
PENNSYLVANIA
JOHN MARSHALL PARK
1st St NW
TAFT MEMORIAL CARILLON
Delaware Av
1st St NE
2nd St NE
Justice Ct
3rd St NE
Frederick Douglass Ct
4th St NE
Constitu
I.R.S.
THE NATIONAL ARCHIVES
FEDERAL TRADE COMM.
Pennsylvania Av
Constitution Av
Constitution Av
A St NE
Millers Ct
5th St NE
E. Capit
Constitution Av
ICE SKATING RINK
NATIONAL GALLERY OF ART
EAST WING NATIONAL GALLERY
Capitol Reflecting Pool
PEACE MONUMENT
THE SUPREME COURT
FOLGER SHAKESPEARE LIBRARY
NATIONAL MUSEUM OF NATURAL HISTORY
Madison Dr
GRANT MONUMENT
U.S. CAPITOL
THE LIBRARY OF CONGRESS
5th St SE
4th St SE
SMITHSONIAN INSTITUTION BUILDING
SCULPTURE GARDEN
ARTS & INDUSTRIES BUILDING
HIRSHHORN MUSEUM
THE MALL
NATIONAL AIR AND SPACE MUSEUM
GARFIELD MONUMENT
ADAMS BUILDING
Indepen
GALLERY
Jefferson Dr
Independence Av
DEPARTMENT OF HEALTH & HUMAN SERVICES
395
U.S. BOTANIC GARDEN
Independence Av
Pennsylvania Av
SACKLER GALLERY
Independence Av
FAA
NASA
DEPARTMENT OF EDUCATION
A St SE
Library Ct
SEWARD SQUARE
NATL. MUSEUM OF AFRICAN ART
DEPT. OF ENERGY
9th St SW
HANCOCK PARK
C St SW
Maryland Av
C St SW
C St SW
C St SW
C St SE
D St SE
New Jersey Av
North Carolina Av
1st St SE
2nd St SE
FOLGER PARK
3rd St SE
D St SE
L'ENFANT PLAZA
7th St SW
D St SW
D St SW
3rd St SW
2nd St SW
1st St SW
Canal St
Ivy St
E St SE
U.S.P.S.
DEPARTMENT OF HOUSING & URBAN DEV.
Virginia Av
School St
4th St SW
E St SW
S. Capitol St
MARIO PARK
12th St SW
L'Enfant Promenade
110th St SW
DEPARTMENT OF TRANSPORTATION
395
Southwest Fwy
Duddington Pl
F St SE
GARFIELD PARK
South Carolina Av
2nd St SE
3rd St SE
4th St SE
5th St SE
Virginia Av
BENJAMIN BANNEKER PARK
Water St SW
G St SW
6th St SW
4th St SW
3rd St SW
H St SW
H St SW
Southeast Fwy
G St SE
2nd St SE
Virginia Av

II ★

During the 1930s Washington, D.C., also grew a great deal. President Franklin D. Roosevelt became president in 1933 in the middle of the Great Depression. This was a time when many people were out of work. Roosevelt wanted to create jobs that would give people work. Because of this, many new government departments were needed to handle the work. With the growth of new departments, more people came to Washington, D.C.

THE MALL

Much of Washington centers on the Mall. The Mall is a large strip of grass about 2 miles (1.6 km) long. It is about three city blocks wide. The Mall goes from the front steps of the Capitol to the edge of the Potomac River just beyond the Lincoln Memorial. The Washington Monument stands in the middle of the Mall, about a mile from the Capitol. Beyond the Monument, and just in front of the Lincoln Memorial, is the Reflecting Pool.

The Mall provides a large space for walking and jogging. During the year, exhibitions and festivals take place there. It is also the place where people come to protest.

THE CAPITOL

The Capitol building is one of Washington's great landmarks. The building is so large that it contains more than 4 acres (1.6 hectares) of floor space. The Capitol has had a long history. It was begun in 1793. During the War of 1812 the British burned the unfinished Capitol to the ground. In 1830, the building was finished, although it has been enlarged over the years.

Both houses of Congress work in the Capitol. The Senate rooms are in the North Wing. The House of Representatives rooms are in the South Wing. The House of Representatives has more rooms than the Senate because the House has four times as many members.

A photo taken of the Capitol while it was being built

The Capitol dome is one of the most famous sights in the city. It rises 287 feet (87 m) from the ground. It has a statue of the Goddess of Freedom at the top. This part of the Capitol was opened in 1863.

A space under the dome links the two sections of the building. This is known as the rotunda. Statuary Hall is to the north of the rotunda. It contains statues and paintings that stand for the 50 states. Statuary Hall is also known as Whispering Hall. You can stand in one corner and whisper to a person in another corner. That person can easily hear your words.

THE WHITE HOUSE

The White House is one of the city's oldest and most famous buildings. It has been home to every president and first family since 1800. George Washington is the only U.S. president who never lived there.

The building was burned by the British, during the War of 1812, but not before First Lady Dolley Madison saved a famous painting of George Washington. In 1817, the building was painted white to hide the stains and soot left by the fire.

Steps lead up to the Capitol building.

First enlarged in 1902, the White House has grown a great deal over the years. It was completely rebuilt between 1948 and 1952.

The president lives and works in the White House. The president works in the Oval Office in the West Wing. The president's wife, known as the First Lady, also works in the White House. There are offices for her and her staff in the East Wing.

The main state rooms are on the first floor of the building. The public may visit these rooms on a tour. The state rooms include the State Dining Room, the East Room, and the Red, Blue, and Green rooms. There are a few other public rooms on the entrance level and on the second floor. The first family's private living quarters take up most of the second and third floors.

The White House from the South Lawn

The Supreme Court building

THE SUPREME COURT

The Supreme Court building was completed in 1935. Before that time, the Supreme Court met in rooms in the Capitol. The current building is made of Vermont marble. Carved into the stone across the front of the building are the words "Equal Justice Under Law." The bronze doors at the entrance weigh 13,000 pounds each. They show the history of the legal system up to the present day.

The eight associate justices and the Chief Justice hear legal cases each year from October until late June or July. Visitors are welcome to attend these sessions. They can also visit the building when the Court is not in session. About 500,000 visitors tour the Supreme Court building each year.

THE WASHINGTON MONUMENT

The city's tallest structure is in the center of the Mall. This is the Washington Monument, which is 555 feet (169 m) tall. It is an obelisk shape. This means that it is a four-sided column that is narrower at the top. A law says that no building taller than the Washington Monument can be built in the city.

The Washington Monument surrounded by cherry blossoms

Work on the monument was begun in 1848, but it took almost 40 years to finish. It opened in 1885. There are 898 steps to the top, but there is also an elevator. At one time it took ten minutes to go by elevator to the top, but now the trip takes just 70 seconds. From the top one can see views in all four directions. Fifty flags fly at the four sides of the base of the monument. These flags are from each of the country's 50 states.

THE LINCOLN MEMORIAL

At the far end of the Mall, almost 2 miles (3.2 km) away from the Capitol, is the Lincoln Memorial. It was dedicated in 1922. It has 36 marble columns that stand for the 36 states that made up the United States when Abraham Lincoln was president.

Inside the memorial is a seated statue of Lincoln by Daniel Chester French. On the wall behind the statue are two famous speeches Lincoln made. These are his Second Inaugural Address and the Gettysburg Address.

(Above) The outside of the Lincoln Memorial
(Below) The famous statue of Lincoln

In 1939 Marian Anderson made history by singing a concert on the steps of the Lincoln Memorial. Because she was African American, the Daughters of the American Revolution (DAR) would not let Anderson sing in Constitution Hall. First Lady Eleanor Roosevelt quickly arranged for the concert to be held at the Lincoln Memorial.

In 1963 more than 200,000 people came to the Lincoln Memorial. They heard Martin Luther King, Jr., deliver his famous "I Have a Dream" speech. In this speech he asked for racial equality for all Americans.

THE JEFFERSON MEMORIAL

Built in honor of our third president, the Jefferson Memorial was completed in 1943, the 200th anniversary of Thomas Jefferson's birth. There is a 19-foot- (5.8-m)-high statue of Jefferson inside the memorial. Words from Jefferson's writings are written on four panels.

Inside the Jefferson Memorial, showing a statue of Jefferson and words taken from the Declaration of Independence

WE HOLD THESE TRUTHS TO BE SELF-EVIDENT: THAT ALL MEN ARE CREATED EQUAL, THAT THEY ARE ENDOWED BY THEIR CREATOR WITH CERTAIN INALIENABLE RIGHTS, AMONG THESE ARE LIFE, LIBERTY AND THE PURSUIT OF HAPPINESS, THAT TO SECURE THESE RIGHTS GOVERNMENTS ARE INSTITUTED AMONG MEN. WE... SOLEMNLY PUBLISH AND DECLARE, THAT THESE COLONIES ARE AND OF RIGH OUGHT TO BE FREE AND INDEPEND TATES...AND FOR THE SUPPORT OF ECLARATION, WITH A FIRM RELI N THE PROTECTION OF D OVIDENCE, WE MUTUALLY PL R LIVES, OUR FORTUNES AND OUR SACRED HONOUR.

Cherry trees bloom every spring around the Tidal Basin. The Jefferson Memorial is in the background.

The Jefferson Memorial overlooks the Tidal Basin. This is a circular inlet of the Potomac River. In the park surrounding the Tidal Basin, cherry trees bloom every spring. These cherry trees were a gift to the United States from the mayor of Tokyo, Japan. President William Howard Taft accepted them in 1912.

THE VIETNAM VETERANS' MEMORIAL

The Vietnam Veterans' Memorial is on the Mall. The Memorial was designed by Maya Ying Lin and opened in 1982. It is made of two black granite walls that are joined to form the letter "V." Together the walls are 525 feet (152.5 m) long. The names of more than 50,000 Americans who fought in Vietnam between 1965 and 1972 are carved in the walls. The soldiers named were either killed or missing in action.

People often place flowers at the Vietnam Veterans' Memorial.

THE SMITHSONIAN INSTITUTION

An English scientist, James Smithson, left his fortune to the United States to build a museum in his name. Today, the Smithsonian is made up of 17 different museums in and around Washington, D.C. It is the largest group of museums in the world.

The Smithsonian also includes the Washington Zoo and Botanical Garden. These popular places are home to animals and plants from around the world.

The original Smithsonian building is known as the Castle. It is now the information center for all the museums. Because the museum owns so many millions of objects, the Smithsonian is often called the nation's attic.

The National Gallery of Art's West Wing has paintings by many famous artists. The recently built East Wing contains many newer pieces of art, including modern American works.

Other parts of the Smithsonian include the National Museum of American History, the National Museum of Natural History, and the Museum of African Art.

The newest Smithsonian addition is the National Museum of the American Indian. The museum will

One of the original Smithsonian buildings, facing the Mall

display art and objects from all the native cultures of the Americas.

The most popular Smithsonian museum is the Air and Space Museum. About eight million people visit it every year. Opened in 1976, the museum is also one of the newest.

At the Air and Space Museum, visitors enjoy seeing rockets and space shuttle equipment.

People come to the Air and Space Museum each year to see the world's first airplane, flown by the Wright Brothers. They can also see Charles Lindbergh's Spirit of St. Louis, in which he flew alone from New York to Paris in 1927, and the first U.S. space capsule.

THE LIBRARY OF CONGRESS

The Library of Congress was originally in the Capitol building. At first, the Library was a research center for members of Congress.

Today the library has about 100 million books and other items. Copies of every book published in the United States are added every day to the collection. As many as 7,000 new items arrive daily. There are more than 535 miles (860 km) of books. The library now stores some items electronically.

The Library of Congress

THE U.S. HOLOCAUST MEMORIAL MUSEUM

The U.S. Holocaust Memorial Museum is one of the city's newest sites. Opened in 1993, nearly two million people visit the museum each year. The site provides for the study of Jewish history, mainly the Holocaust period of World War II. This is the time when more than six million Jews died in Europe.

Each visitor to the museum receives an identity card upon entering. This card has the name and information about a person who was a victim of the Holocaust. It helps to give the visitor a sense of the history of the time. There is also a computer learning center. There visitors can try to find names of family members who died during the Holocaust.

Visitors study pictures of Holocaust victims at the U.S. Holocaust Memorial Museum.

The Kennedy Center, set on the Potomac River

THE KENNEDY CENTER

The Kennedy Center for the Performing Arts is a popular site in Washington, D.C., for all kinds of entertainment. The building is named in honor of President John F. Kennedy. The center is built along the Potomac River, just northwest of the Lincoln Memorial. World-famous performers present plays, ballet, modern dance, opera, concerts, and other musical performances. There are three different theaters at the Kennedy Center.

FORD'S THEATER

Ford's Theater is the small 19th-century playhouse where actor John Wilkes Booth shot President Abraham Lincoln. Lincoln was attending a play with his wife, Mary Todd Lincoln. Ford's Theater is still used today for some plays. People may visit it as well.

Inside Ford's Theater, showing the box where Lincoln was sitting when he was shot

NATIONAL CATHEDRAL

The founders of the United States dreamed of a church for all Americans. It was to be used by people of all religions.

Work on the National Cathedral was begun in 1907. The cathedral was finally finished in 1990. It is the sixth largest cathedral in the world. It has more than 200 stained glass windows. One of the windows has rocks from the moon in the glass. American plants and animals are carved into the many stones on the inside and outside of the building.

National Cathedral

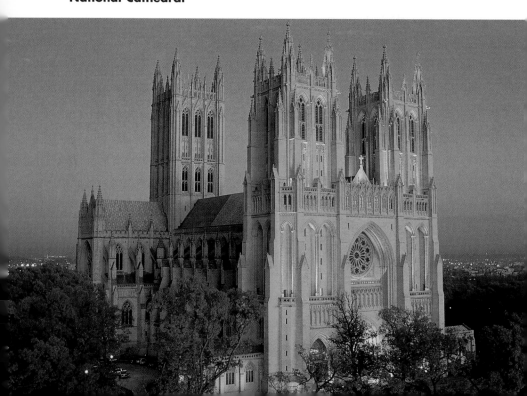

A view of the Pentagon from above

THE PENTAGON

The National Defense Building stands less than a mile from the city, across the Potomac River in Arlington, Virginia. It is also known as the Pentagon, because it has five sides. It is a large building with wings that enclose a five-sided courtyard. The Pentagon is headquarters for the Department of Defense, which oversees all of the U.S. Armed Forces. These include the Army, the Navy and Marines, and the Air Force.

ARLINGTON NATIONAL CEMETERY

Close to the Pentagon is Arlington National Cemetery. In this quiet place lie 60,000 Americans who died fighting for their country. The cemetery also contains the Tomb of the Unknowns. This is a memorial that honors all members of the U.S. armed forces who have died in wars. Also in the cemetery is the grave of President John F. Kennedy. The grave is simple and has a flame that always burns.

A guard in uniform marches past the Tomb of the Unknowns.

SOME OTHER
WASHINGTON HIGHLIGHTS

The National Archives building faces the Mall. This
large building has the original Declaration of
Independence, Constitution, and Bill of Rights. They are
displayed in glass cases. The cases can be lowered and
hidden below ground quickly if needed in the event of an
enemy attack.

Washington, D.C. is the home of the Treasury. The
Treasury Building dates from 1842 and is one of the
oldest buildings in the city. The Treasury manages the
Bureau of Engraving and Printing. This is the place
where bills are printed and coins are minted.

(Above) The inside of the National Archives
(Below) The Treasury Building

Another landmark is Union Station. Built in 1907 of gleaming white marble, this enormous railroad station was rebuilt in 1988. It is still the main train station for the capital. Now there are food courts, fine restaurants, and even a movie theater complex. The Metro also stops at Union Station. These sleek new subway trains take people to almost any part of the city.

Union Station

Washington, D.C., has a modern subway system, known as the Metro.

Printing and publishing are important industries in Washington, D.C. The Government Printing Office (GPO) is the world's largest printer. And the daily newspaper, *The Washington Post*, is the city's single largest business employer.

Because Washington is the nation's capital, the governments of nearly every nation in the world have offices there. They are known as embassies. Many of them are located along Massachusetts Avenue. Because of this, the street is known as Embassy Row.

Many students attend the city's colleges and universities. Georgetown University is known for its schools of law and government. Howard University is well known for its research centers and modern laboratories. The student body is largely African American. Gallaudet University is one of the world's leading centers for students who are deaf.

The Capitol at night

HOW THE DISTRICT IS GOVERNED

Congress oversees the local government of Washington, D.C., and can make its own laws for the city. Congress can veto laws passed by the city council, too. The chief executive of Washington's city government is the mayor. The mayor is elected every four years. The mayor presides over a 13-member city council that makes the city's laws.

The District of Columbia has one representative in the House of Representatives. This representative may listen to discussions. But this person is not allowed to vote in the House. There are no senators from Washington, D.C.

WASHINGTON TOMORROW

Many people who live in Washington, D.C., would like the city to become the country's 51st state. There is sometimes talk about making the District of Columbia a state. Washington holds a special position. It has been the nation's capital for more than 200 years. Many people think it should remain this way and not become a state.

Washington is a city where many important decisions are made. It is the home of landmarks linked to the past, present, and future of the United States. It was a new city when the nation was new. It has grown as our country has grown. And ever since it was built, it has belonged to all citizens of our country.

Glossary

Capital A city that is the center of government

Capitol The building in which the U.S. Congress meets

Chief justice The head judge of the Supreme Court

Congress The lawmaking branch of the United States

District An area or region

Dome A large round roof or ceiling

Embassy The official residence or office of an ambassador

Engraving Words or pictures etched into a hard surface

First Lady The wife of the president of the United States

Landmark An important building or structure

Pentagon The headquarters of the Department of Defense

Representative A member of the House of Representatives

Rotunda An area under the dome of the Capitol building

Senator A member of the U.S. Senate

State Rooms Large public rooms in the White House

Supreme Court The highest court in the United States

Veto To refuse to sign a bill into law

Index